Hello, Beautiful!

Water Animals

WORLD
BOOK

www.worldbook.com

World Book, Inc.
180 North LaSalle Street, Suite 900
Chicago, Illinois 60601
USA

For information about other World Book publications, visit our website at www.worldbook.com or call 1-800-WORLDBK (967-5325).

For information about sales to schools and libraries, call 1-800-975-3250 (United States), or 1-800-837-5365 (Canada).

Library of Congress Cataloging-in-Publication Data for this volume has been applied for.

Hello, Beautiful!
ISBN: 978-0-7166-3567-3 (set, hc.)

Water Animals
ISBN: 978-0-7166-3576-5 (hc.)

Also available as:
ISBN: 978-0-7166-3586-4 (e-book)

Printed in China by Shenzhen Wing King Tong Paper Products Co., Ltd., Shenzhen, Guangdong
1st printing July 2018

Staff

Contents

Introduction

Welcome to "Hello, Beautiful!" picture books!

This book is about animals that live in or near the water. Each book in the "Hello, Beautiful!" series uses large, colorful photographs and a few words to describe our world to children who are not yet reading on their own or are beginning to learn to read. For the benefit of both grown-up and child readers, a picture key is included in the back of the volume to describe each photograph and specific type of animal in more detail.

"Hello, Beautiful!" books can help pre-readers and starting readers get into the habit of having fun with books and learning from them, too. With pre-readers, a grown-up reader (parent, grandparent, librarian, teacher, older brother or sister) can point to the words on each page as he or she speaks them aloud to help the listening child associate the concept of text with the object or idea it describes.

Large, colorful photographs give pre-readers plenty to see while they listen to the reader. If no reader is available, pre-readers can "read" on their own, turning the pages of the book and speaking their own stories about what they see. For new readers, the photographs provide visual hints about the words on the page. Often, these words describe the specific type of animal shown. This animal may not be representative of all species, or types, of that animal.

This book displays some of the spectacular animals that dive, splash, or paddle through the world's oceans, lakes, and rivers. Bodies of water are frequently polluted, which endangers the animals that live within them. Help inspire respect and care for these important and beautiful animals by sharing this "Hello, Beautiful!" book with a child soon.

Bird

Hello, beautiful bird!

You are a Wilson's storm-petrel.

You are a kind of ocean bird.
Your feathers are black.
There are white feathers
in a line across your tail.

You fly down to scoop things to
eat from the water's surface!

Cod

Hello, beautiful cod!

You are a potato cod.

The dark spots on your body are shaped a bit like potatoes!

You are a friendly fish that likes to swim with divers!

Dolphin

Hello, beautiful dolphin!

You are a bottlenose dolphin.

You swim in the water like a fish, but you are not a fish. You need to put your head out of the water to breathe air.

You are a smart, smiling animal!

Lobster

Hello, beautiful lobster!

You are an American lobster.

You have a hard shell to protect your body.

You use your two big claws to catch other animals to eat.

Octopus

Hello, beautiful octopus!

You are a North Pacific giant octopus.

You have eight long arms and a big, soft body.

You can squirt an inky liquid to hide yourself!

Penguin

Hello, beautiful penguin!

You are an Adélie penguin.

You have wings, but you cannot fly. You use them to swim through the water!

You waddle on land on your short legs!

Sea anemone

Hello, beautiful sea anemone!

You look like a colorful flower, but you are an animal! You may be pink, blue, green, or red.

You catch small animals to eat with your feelers.

Sea turtle

Hello, beautiful
sea turtle!

You are a leatherback sea turtle.

Your dark skin has white
spots.

You live most of your life in
the ocean. Your large flippers
make you a great swimmer!

Shark

Hello, beautiful shark!

You are a great white shark.

You have many sharp teeth.

You swim through the ocean very fast!

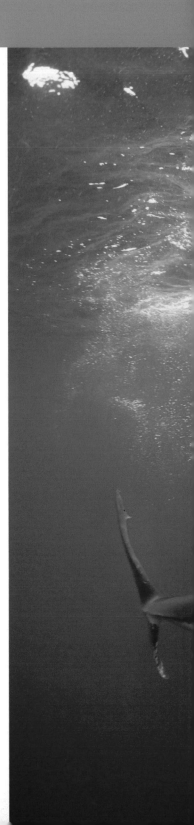

22

Stingray

Hello, beautiful stingray!

You are a kind of fish. You have a flat body and a long, skinny tail.

Your dark color helps you hide on the ocean floor!

Trout

Hello, beautiful trout!

You are a **brown** trout.

Your body is marked with dark spots.

People love to fish for you! Get away from that hook!

Whale

Hello, beautiful whale!

You are a Bryde's whale.

Like a dolphin, you are not a fish. You breathe air through a hole on the top of your head.

You are one of the smartest animals on Earth!

Picture Key

Find out more about these water animals! Use the picture keys below to learn where each animal lives, how big it grows, and its favorite foods!

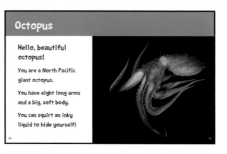

Pages 6-7 Bird
The Wilson's storm-petrel *(PEHT ruhl)* visits oceans around the world. It grows to 7 inches (18 centimeters) long. Wilson's storm-petrels eat small crustaceans, including shrimp, small fish, and other small animals.

Pages 8-9 Cod
The potato cod is found mainly in coastal waters of the Indian and western Pacific oceans. They live among coral reefs and move around the bottom of the reefs looking for food. Potato cod grow to 6 ½ feet (2 meters) long and can weigh up to 220 pounds (100 kilograms). Potato cod eat a variety of reef animals, including small rays and other fish, crabs, squid, octopuses, and spiny lobsters.

Pages 10-11 Dolphin
The bottlenose dolphin lives in warm to tropical ocean waters, typically within 100 miles (160 kilometers) of land. They can be found off the coast of Florida, as far north as the waters of Japan and Norway, and as far south as Argentina, New Zealand, and South Africa. Bottlenose dolphins measure up to 13 feet (4 meters) long and can weigh as much as 600 pounds (272 kilograms). Dolphins eat fish and squid.

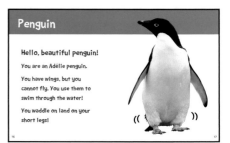

Pages 12-13 Lobster
American lobsters live on sandy, muddy, or rocky bottom areas near the coast of the Atlantic Ocean. They can measure as long as 42 inches (107 centimeters) and weigh nearly 45 pounds (20 kilograms). However, most lobsters are caught before they reach full size. Captured lobsters generally measure about 8 inches (30 centimeters) long and weigh only about 1 pound (0.45 kilogram) or less. They eat algae, plants called eelgrass, clams, crab, snails, small fish, and even other lobsters.

Pages 14-15 Octopus
The North Pacific giant octopus lives near the bottom of the Pacific Ocean. It can weigh up to 150 pounds (68 kilograms). It measures more than 20 feet (6 meters) from the tip of one arm to the tip of another on the opposite side of the body. The North Pacific giant octopus feeds on clams, crabs, lobsters, snails, fish, and even other octopuses.

Pages 16-17 Penguin
The Adélie *(uh DAY lee)* penguin lives in Antarctica and the surrounding Southern Ocean. It stands about 18 inches (46 centimeters) tall and weighs 8 ½ to 12 pounds (4 to 5.5 kilograms). The Adélie penguin eats mainly shrimplike krill.

Sea anemone

Hello, beautiful sea anemone!

You look like a colorful flower, but you are an animal! You may be pink, blue, green, or red.

You catch small animals to eat with your feelers.

Sea turtle

Hello, beautiful sea turtle!

You are a leatherback sea turtle.

Your dark skin has white spots.

You live most of your life in the ocean. Your large flippers make you a great swimmer!

Shark

Hello, beautiful shark!

You are a great white shark.

You have many sharp teeth.

You swim through the ocean very fast!

Pages 18-19 Sea anemone
Sea anemones *(uh NEHM uh neez)* live throughout the world's oceans. They measure from ¼ inch (6 millimeters) to over 3 feet (90 centimeters) in diameter. Sea anemones eat small *invertebrates* (animals without backbones) and even fish.

Pages 20-21 Sea turtle
The leatherback sea turtle is found primarily in the open ocean, as far north as Alaska, Canada, and Iceland, and as far south as the southern tip of Africa. The largest turtle, leatherbacks grow from 4 to 8 feet (1.2 to 2.4 meters) long and weigh up to 2,000 pounds (900 kilograms). Leatherbacks chiefly eat jellyfish.

Pages 22-23 Shark
The great white shark lives in the coastal areas of cool oceans throughout the world. They can grow to more than 21 feet (6.4 meters) in length. Great white sharks primarily prey on seals and sea lions.

Stingray

Hello, beautiful stingray!

You are a kind of fish. You have a flat body and a long, skinny tail.

Your dark color helps you hide on the ocean floor!

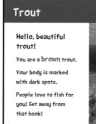

Trout

Hello, beautiful trout!

You are a brown trout.

Your body is marked with dark spots.

People love to fish for you! Get away from that hook!

Whale

Hello, beautiful whale!

You are a Bryde's whale.

Like a dolphin, you are not a fish. You breathe air through a hole on the top of your head.

You are one of the smartest animals on Earth!

Pages 24-25 Stingray
Most stingrays live on sandy to muddy bottoms in shallow parts of the ocean and in bays. The largest stingrays can grow up to 6 ½ feet (2 meters) across and weigh up to 1300 pounds (600 kilograms). Stingrays prey on clams, oysters, crabs, mussels, and a variety of other animals.

Pages 26-27 Trout
The brown trout is native to Europe and western Asia, but has been introduced throughout North America. Most grow to about 10 inches (25 centimeters) long. Young trout eat mainly invertebrates, including insects. Mature trout also feed on other fish and on crayfish.

Pages 28-29 Whale
The Bryde's *(BROO duhs)* whale lives in tropical and subtropical seas. It is not found in waters that are colder than 59 °F (15 °C). A Bryde's whale may reach about 45 feet (14 meters) in length. Bryde's whales eat mainly squid and small fish.

Index